C000160505

KNIFE EDGE

Bancroft

ISBN: 978-1-915079-17-6

Cover designed by Aaron Kent

Edited and typeset by Aaron Kent

Broken Sleep Books Ltd
Rhydwen,
Talgarreg,
SA44 4HB
Wales

Contents

For Donna, who saved my life.

Knife Edge

Colin Bancroft

A man was stabbed in the back in Castleton at about 5.15pm yesterday (Tuesday 9 February). The 26-year-old man is now in hospital having also suffered a suspected tear to his liver as a result of the stabbing. The victim was on Scholes Street, near to a garage, when he felt an ache in the right hand side of his back. When he turned round, he found he had been stabbed in the back, possibly by a kitchen knife with a white handle. The offender then fled onto Lennon Street. He is described as white, about 5ft 9in to 5ft 10in tall, of skinny build and wearing a black cap, a dark blue or black hooded top covering the cap and dark shell suit trousers. The victim remains in hospital in a serious condition. Detectives in Rochdale are now appealing to anyone with information to come forward.

— Rochdale Online: 10th February 2010

Education at Her Majesty's Leisure

From Carol Ann Duffy

You touch my arm. But before I turn
You stab me in the back. A sneak attack
Like when Macbeth wet up Duncan in his bed.
You think that you are death and I am dead.
But I give chase. Imagine the look on the face
Of Tybalt when Romeo flipped and lost his shit
Before he stuck that blade between his ribs.
That was it. But in this production
I am Mercutio, dealt a mortal blow as I stagger
Into the Co-op and collapse on the floor.
Old Hamlet's ghost. Almost. [*Later that night*]
I wake in a darkened room. A tomb. Alone.
Hermione's slow return from stone.
And you, Claudius in your cell, babbling
Your confession. That bullshit apology,
How you'd learnt your lesson.

Notes on what to expect if you're stabbed

As the knife enters your body
Your muscles will contract
And you'll release air like a burst balloon.
There will be a sharp intake of breath,
Your body will stiffen like clay in the sun.

Please remember this:
You will not bleed out like in the movies,
Your shirt will not be dyed in an instant.
Your life will edge off slowly,
Like a prisoner sensitising to light.

Did you know that everything turns purple when you die?

The blade entered my back:

[Epidermis, dermis, hypodermis, iliocostalis, longissimus, spinalis, right lung, liver - shredded]

For a moment the world paused. Then I saw it, a shark on a white handle. He turned to rubber neck my disaster. The surprise in his eyes as I gave chase. My head swam. Adrenalin propping up collapsing revetments. The security guard in the Co-op didn't have a clue what to do. Stabbing not in the training manual. I called the ambulance myself, babbling as the world shrank around me. Everything seen through a fish eye lens like some nineties hip-hop video. She led me inside, took the phone, laid me on the floor. People carried on shopping. *[What thoughts I have of you tonight, Walt Whitman]* The ambulance took forever. I coughed up verbs. Strange constellations flowered before my eyes, psychedelic supernovas and spinning kaleidoscopes in the cereal aisle.

Did you know that everything turns purple when you die?

Sirens broke the silence. An oxygen mask redrew my world. Outside/sunlight/evaporating/dusk. A hundred eyes watched my departure, someone took a selfie. A policeman taped off the road like a giant birthday present.

Liutprand

The first hourglass, or sand clock, is said to have been invented by a French monk called Liutprand in the 8th century AD

The scriptorium stank of tallow
And the light wasn't really light;
More of a shifting blackness
That guttered against the walls.
He sat alone, making time,
His hands warping wood around
A bulb of glass filled with powdered
Marble, as if the pillars of time
Were ground to dust.
Bottling eternity. *Aeon.*
Until he forced it a little too hard,
And the glass rifted. Cracking
Radially, the way stars form
At night, splintering darkness.
The silt spilt through, running
To the floor – unfettered –
He tried to hold the broken
Jigsaw in place, gauze over a wound.
His hands, poised like mine that night,
Sealing a hole after the knife withdrew,
Feeling time

       slip,

           slip,

               slip

                    through my fingers.

Gravelet Traverses Niagara

Let's be honest: none of the five thousand
Strong crowd gathered on the cliff edge
Were there to watch him make it to the other side.
What they secretly wanted was for him to topple
From the wire and fall hundreds of feet
Through the air, spinning and twisting
Like an eddy to the bottom of the gorge,
His body breaking on the rocks
As though it were made of waves.

But he felt none of that as he concentrated
On putting one foot in front of the other,
Felt the wind buffet his body
As though he were a pendulum on borrowed time,
His life in the balance of a pole in his hands
That tilted rhythmically, a set of scales weighing
Up his fate as he walked the finest of lines,
That had never before, nor would ever again,
Be so clearly defined.

Bystander Effect

I lay on the floor of the Co-op. Tiles cold against my face, as though the ice spreading through my body was seeping up from the ground. There was a dockyard of shoes in front of me, each facing the same way, like compasses pointing north. Shelves towered above me like billboards. Someone stepped over me to get to the soup tins. How strange it was, watching those people do their shopping, showing only a passing interest in the collapsed body on the floor, as though it were something only slightly out of the norm for a Tuesday Night.

It had been in the fence for an hour, its bleats echoing from the wood. I'd seen it from the kitchen window and thought that the farmer would be down to free it at any moment. But it was getting late. I threw on my coat and boots and trudged across the field. The pheasants chucking off theatrically. When it heard me coming it thrashed around in panic. Rain lashed sideways from the moor, stinging my face. I grabbed it behind its neck and untwisted the wire that had tightened like a noose. It was away. Sirening off into the twilight, the rest of the flock looking up for a moment, before going back to their grazing.

Noodle Brain

I finished it twenty minutes before it happened,
Bombay Badboy. Not the last meal
That I had imagined, but who knows
                              when the end is the end?
What I remember about the drive in the ambulance
Wasn't the pain or procedures, but the thought
That you would get home and find the pot
On the countertop, left out of laziness as usual,
And silently curse me for not doing what you ask.
And I couldn't deal with that curse then,
Not at that moment when I needed you most.
Maybe the reason why I haven't had one since
Is because it looks like a dried-out brain,
And the sudden shock of the hot water stirs
It all to life again,
                    the sachet of sauce
                              ripped open like a wound.

Prometheus

They said I was stupid when I said that I saw
Prometheus out on the moor.
But I'd seen those birds before, not eagles
but kites, circling, ready to bite
To slash at his liver, his heart.
I knew because I've been torn apart
By similar things – spectral wraiths
On ghostly wings that stab at insides.
I knew it was him when I saw the sliver
Of light in the night. Not a torch
But a mote, remote in its glow.
Like me in the dark of the hospital ward,
Clinging to life, ready to go.

Holding it all Together

My skin has been planed
                                    back
Stripped to woodwork

Doors that should
            never be opened
Hands   feet
                        cold blue stones
They do not feel
                    as if they are mine.
Some junction of my brain is
                                    bro

                                                ken

Vein walls
            collapse
            old mine shafts
Blood a   heavy glue
I stop start into uneasy rest
            Each breath drags on
My lung a shredded tyre
The wound on my back
Patched together
Everything down to the wire

Calpurnia

I have never asked what those hours were like
In that limbo as you prepared tea, watched TV,
Unwound yourself from your day.
Did you know that something was off?
Could you feel the tilt of the axis swinging
Away from our centre? I couldn't.
There were no signs, no warnings given
Of impending doom, no comets seen,
No lionesses whelped in the streets
As in Rome, no ghosts shrieked and squealed.
I remember waking and seeing you
Curled in the chair at the bedside, exhausted
No doubt by the trauma, the rush of not knowing
What had happened, or why you were now in exile,
Displaced from our life in the moments before
To the one after that knock on the door.

Delusions of Glass

Sometimes I feel as though I am made of glass.
As though I have been blown together
From the silica of a dried-up sea.
Not stained glass church windows
Flashing brilliant reds and greens at sunset,
But translucent glass that light passes
Through akilter, casting unrefined
Ribbons of colour in my wake.
The edges of my fingers are sharp, cutting,
My tongue a dagger. Watch me as I walk,
Rattling in my panes. Can you see the vibrations?
The small chip underneath my rib,
An imperfection that will grow to a crack,
A schism, splitting me apart.

Worried to Death

I hadn't heard anything in the night
And I didn't know anything was amiss
Until I went out to feed them
And found them scattered across the yard.
There was no blood, each one
Could have been asleep, but for the rigidity
Of their bodies after a night out in the cold.
You said someone must have let them out
On purpose, baited them for fun,
That they had been worried to death -
But I couldn't comprehend such a thing then.
I didn't understand why I heard nothing,
Being so close, almost under their noses.
How could I not have heard Death so rampant?
I saw that exact look in your eye again
When you stood, shaking, over my bed
Asking me what had happened, who had done what.
Why. I held your hand and told you;
How I had simply been there, minding my own,
Before he plunged the knife into my back,
The cold shock, the pointlessness -
How all I could remember, was silence.

Revelations

The rabbit was a flesh wound on the road.
Stupidly pink against the black tarmac,
Its body flattened into a blancmange
Of organ and fat. The impact had turned
It inside out, its inner workings exposed
To air and light for the first and only time.
A sacred, secret darkness unlocked:
Something that once it was let out
Could never be put back in its box.

Augur

It doesn't know how close it is to death
As it pecks the seeds beneath the trees
Scattered from the feeders by the tits.
It doesn't know that just beyond the copse
Stand men with guns, the last hunt of the year.
I want to warn it, shout out for it to fly
In any direction but the one where it will die.
But how do you become animal intuition?
Become a premonition in a language you don't speak?
If I knew I might have read the signs
Myself the night I almost lost my life.
Heard the magpies call from the telephone lines
Or read the cloud formations in the sky.
Maybe there are things that we shouldn't know,
That are best left up to chaos to decide,
Because we'd never leave the house at all
But lock the door and find a place to hide.

Voldemort

Ever since I watched that scene at the end of *Goblet of Fire*, I have called it Voldemort. You know the one, where Harry and Diggory have just triumphed in the maze and have grabbed the port key, thinking they've won the Tri-Wizard Tournament and eternal glory before they are transported to that graveyard. From there it all goes to pot. Diggory is wiped out and Harry is pinned to that gravestone while Wormtail goes through the ritual to bring you-know-who back to life. I find it funny that those ingredients – the bones of a father, the flesh of a follower and even one's own blood can conjure up something that you thought you had beaten. But here it is again, in all its pomp and swagger, fully robed, crucifying for pleasure in a graveyard where even the echoes of loved ones can't do shit about the fact that it is back, that it never died, that it's letting you know it can touch you now.

Death Wish

Fuck it became the motto because I knew I couldn't die. I had a recurring impulse as I crossed the motorway bridge to scramble down the bank and walk across all six lanes of rush hour traffic because I knew nothing would happen. One night I closed my eyes and counted to fifteen as I balanced on my tiptoes on top of the carpark roof. I went down dark alleyways searching for the truth but nothing dared jump from the shadows, and when a fight kicked off outside the pub I stood amongst the melee without a scratch. But being indestructible eventually messed with my head because I had no idea why I was still here, and I wished Death would just show up so I could ascertain the facts of why the fuck he decided to send me back. I finally realised as I watched the news that June as Derrick Bird rampaged through Cumbria, all those people in the wrong place at the wrong time, that there was no design, that that might be all that life is, just a succession of near misses, deflections of catastrophe that can turn any way in an instant, a stray decision that means the difference between walking away unscathed or being wrecked by the collision.

Scar

I stood on the hill looking down into the valley
at the heaps of slag dumped on the edge
Of the quarry, the mounds piled high like the barrows
Of Neolithic kings robbed of their mineral robes.
     The old pump house was a ruin of stone,
The roof long lost and the tops of the walls covered
In a thick baize of moss, a hollowed-out snooker table.
     I skied down the scree slope,
The ground moving quickly underneath my feet,
A dry hushing. I peered through the gate that blocked
The adit, the passageway filled with water and the echo
Of my voice as I called out to the dark.
     Walking back to the tops,
Through new growths of beech and ash,
Foxgloves, speedwell, the mottled rash
Of cranesbill climbing up the bank,
I revelled in the regeneration.
     But one turn of the wind
And a switch in the waves of the grass revealed
An enormous scar running horizontally along
The ridge, barren except for the shadows
Of the scrambling grass. I reached around
To my back, knowing it is something
We share, these rifts on our landscapes
       That can never be hidden,
       That will always be there,
       No matter how many layers we wear.

Sun Dial

During summer the late afternoon
Light falls through the backroom window
And lays squares of heat across the bed,
An illuminated chessboard on which I
Throw myself down like a conquered King,
In a daily ritual of abandonment.
Each day the light shifts imperceptibly,
Climbing higher up the wall, before
Receding from the high-tide marks of summer,
Until by this mid-winter afternoon,
It has barely cracked the floor beyond the sill.
And there it will flatline for days, in stasis,
A golden thread as thin as the edge of a knife
Until suddenly something shifts it back into life

Irredenta

'Dark house, by which I once more stand'
— Tennyson

This street was once a part of my lore,
Hachured cobbles mapping out its camber,
The dark woodland of oddly numbered doors
And the windows softly shifting amber.

Terraced houses, Victorian back to backs
Clinging grimly to the incline of the hill.
Ruderal flowers, squatting in the cracks
Between the garages, hanging on still.

I walk past our old house, the door ajar,
The walls behind a different shade of blue,
The driveway with a foreign car:
Everything familiar, but new.

Crackle

She knocked with a finger
The way one does at the door of an empty
House. The dull thud of an echo
As she laid the stethoscope
On my back like a safe cracker
And listened, shifting the diaphragm,
Searching for the right spot,
The right amount of hollow.
"There's a slight crackle" she said,
Straining to hear,
Like a marooned woman glued to a wireless,
Turning through frequencies,
                        intermittently receiving
Some form of code, slowly revealing
              a rescue,
                    a healing.

Aberdeen

Thinking back, it was a mad idea
To go up to that top corner shelf
Of land in such precarious health,
Just four weeks after the stabbing;
My skin a translucent parchment,
My body a bag of broken ornaments.
We didn't appreciate how far
It was that morning we jumped in the car.
But we had to escape the claustrophobia
Of home, the interview the perfect excuse.
Neither of us said but we both knew I hadn't
A chance of getting in: frail, shuffling shade
Of my former self. More junkie than teacher.

Our premonition turning out to be true.

I was morose on the way back home,
Angry, anchored in misery, black clouds.
When you pulled in at Tyrebagger
To empty the car of my weather
I told you to just go, to leave me there,
That you would be better off on your own,
Before the freezing February air,
Lethal on my lung, had me coughing up
Sorrys on the edge of the wood where snowdrops
Had blanked out every inch of the ground,
A clean slate, Spring's latest shot at life,
And you stood next to me, taking my hand,
Telling me that everything would be all right.

Acknowledgements

'Bystander Effect' & 'Scars' were first published in *Poetry Birmingham Literary Journal*.

'Prometheus' was first published in *Eye Flash*.

'Delusions of Glass' was first published in *Cannon's Mouth*.

'Worried to Death' was first published in *Poets' Republic*.

'Augur' was first published in *Anthropocene*.

'Notes on what to expect if you're stabbed' was first published in *Sledgehammer*.

Lay Out Your Unrest

Lightning Source UK Ltd.
Milton Keynes UK
UKHW011819080422
401288UK00002B/139